Scandinavian Proverbs

A Life without Love is like a year without summer.

Collected by Julie Jensen McDonald

Edited by Joan Liffring-Zug

Calligraphy by Esther Feske

Penfield
Press

The Author

Julie Jensen McDonald was born in Audubon County, Iowa. Her mother's parents emigrated from Denmark in the 1880's, and her father came from Denmark when he was 19.

A graduate of the University of Iowa, Mrs. McDonald is the author of nine published books, including a Danish-American trilogy of novels. She is a lecturer in journalism at St. Ambrose College, Davenport, Iowa, and a participant in the Iowa Arts Council's Writers-in-the-Schools program.

The Calligrapher

Esther Feske, M.F.A. graduate of the University of Iowa, is a calligrapher and graphic designer in Albuquerque, New Mexico.

More Books

For a complete list of our Scandinavian books, write to Penfield Press
215 Brown St.
Iowa City, IA 52240

© 1985 Penfield Press

All rights reserved. Illustrations and text may not be reproduced without written approval of Penfield Press except for a review of the book.
Printed by Julin Printing Co., Monticello, Iowa 52310, on acid-free paper. ∞
ISBN 0-941016-26-9 cloth
ISBN 0-941016-27-7 paper

On Gathering Proverbs

When I began the research for my trilogy of Danish-American novels, I came across a proverb that seemed like the lucky almond in the Christmas pudding and tucked it away for future use. "Don't sail out farther than you can row back" eventually gave me the title for the third book, *The Sailing Out*. Other proverbs helped me understand the character of the Danes.

Later I worked on a Swedish-American novel, and I found more proverbs with a slightly different flavor. I became curious about the folk wisdom of the rest of Scandinavia and spent happy hours browsing in the fine Scandinavian collection at Augustana College, Rock Island, Illinois. This pleasurable activity went on in countless other libraries in several states, and it was more like picking wild strawberries than serious research. I added my harvest to the proverbs passed down by family and friends.

The Swedes contend that "a proverb says what all people think," and I have tried to remove the barrier of archaic language in this collection. This effort will account for the slight alteration of "what Grandma used to say."

A proverb is defined as "a short, wise saying used for a long time by many people." It may comfort or deplore, mock or praise, and it fingerprints the national character of its creator.

The Nordic soul gives a special flavor to the adage, and while the nations of Scandinavia are distinctly varied, they share the solid good sense that makes a proverb endure.

Because my own background is Danish, the short, sharp and shiny sayings of that country are most familiar to me, but I find the same wry practicality in the proverbs of other Scandinavian nations, the same quicksilver feeling.

The Danes are the grace notes in the music of Scandinavia, relieving the heavy themes of life with the light touch. They walk the tightrope of the Golden Mean, blending fairy-tale flights of fancy with bacon-and-eggs pragmatism.

The Finns, descended from Shamanistic nomads, carry the *Kalevala*, the national epic of prehistoric Finland, close to their hearts. They are credited with early use of the log cabin, a shelter from the wild nature that inspired their chief composer, Sibelius.

Icelanders bear traces of the Irish, who discovered their island before 800 A.D. The first settlers were the Norsemen, primarily Norwegians. Heroic sagas and Eddic and skaldic poetry are in the blood of these inhabitants of a land of volcanoes and geysers.

Norwegians have an ancient culture dating from 12,000 B.C., but they were unknown to the rest of the world until the Viking jarls began to raid the coasts of Europe in the ninth century A.D. The staunch character of the people has been forged by the rigorous geography of their homeland, and their arts reflect the sea, the earth and the mountains.

Swedes love beauty, but they want it to be useful. Their arts are practical and real. However, a stern climate turns the people to their inner weather, and they are experienced at cultivating the loneliness of their souls. Swedish filmmaker Ingmar Bergman is unrivaled in the exploration of that terrain. A rich epic literature existed in Sweden until the Christian era, when it was destroyed because it was pagan.

Here, then, are the short bits of wisdom conceived in a cold climate. The proverbs undoubtedly lose something in translation,

but they remain an Aurora Borealis of
northern insights.

Julie Jensen McDonald

Better thin beer than an empty jug

Danish Proverb

Judge a maiden
   at the kneading trough,
   not at the dance.

-Danish

A sip at a time
   empties the cask.

-Norwegian

Food tastes best
   when you eat it
   with your own spoon.

-Danish

A sitting crow starves.

-Icelandic

When it rains soup,
     the poor man
     has no spoon.

-Swedish

A piece of bread
   in the pocket
   is better than
a feather in the hat.

-Swedish

When the manger is empty,
the horses bite each other.

-Danish

A fool
is like other folks
as long as he's silent.

-Danish

If there were no fools,
how would we recognize
the wise?

-Norwegian

*He who would make
a fool of himself
finds many
to help him.*

-Danish

*Spite
is an early riser.*

-Swedish

He who does not go to church
in bad weather
will go to hell
when it's fair.

-Finnish

When sin drives,
shame sits in the back seat.

-Swedish

He who is too pleasing
to himself
is displeasing to others.

-Danish

He who comes last sees least.

-Norwegian

Mediocrity
is climbing molehills without sweating.

-Icelandic

An old error
has more friends
than a new truth.

-Danish

He who praises the past
blames the present.

-Finnish

The horse one cannot have
has every fault.

-Danish

Envy shoots at others and wounds itself.

-Swedish

No one becomes a good doctor before he fills a churchyard.

-Swedish

On the gallows, the first night is the worst.

-Finnish

WORRY
often
gives a
small
thing
a big
shadow.

-Swedish proverb

Gifts should be handed,
not hurled.

-Danish

He who gives to me
teaches me to give.

-Danish

God gives every bird its food
but does not
drop it
into
the nest.

-Danish

He who buys
what he doesn't need
steals from himself.

-Swedish

The perpetual saver
always lives in poverty.

-Danish

It's no disgrace to be poor,
but it can be inconvenient.

-Danish

That which is desired
by many
is owned by few.

-Danish

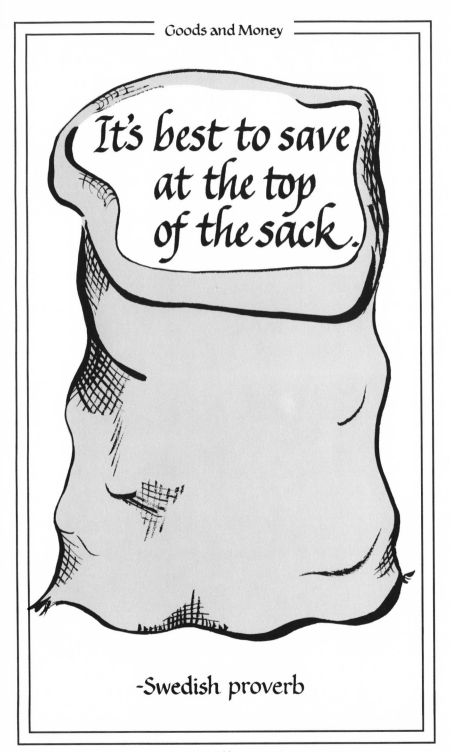

It's best to save
at the top
of the sack.

-Swedish proverb

Don't throw away
the old bucket until
you're sure the new
one holds water.

-Swedish

Let no one see
what is in your heart
                    or your purse.

-Danish

He who knows how to beg
may leave his purse at home.

-Danish

One sits best
on one's own bench.

-Norwegian

hope
is the dream
of waking.

-Danish

Things never go so well
that one should have
no fear
nor so ill
that one should have
no hope.

-Danish

Even a blind hen
finds a grain occasionally.

-Finnish

The word
that lies nearest the heart
comes first to the lips.

-Norwegian

You may go
where you wish,
but you cannot
escape yourself.

-Norwegian

One should speak
little with others and
much with oneself.

-Danish

Nobody sighs deeper
than those who have no troubles.

-Norwegian

You may light
another's candle
at your own
without loss.

-Danish

That man is to be pitied
who never is envied.

-Icelandic

Heroism
consists of hanging on
one minute longer.

-Norwegian

What you cannot say
briefly
you do not know.

-Danish

The road
to a
friend's
house is
never long.

-Danish

When there is room in the heart,
there is room in the house.

-Danish

A linen shirt
sewn by one's mother
is warmer than
a woolen cloak
sewn by a stranger.

-Finnish

That which is loved
is always beautiful.

-Norwegian

A life without love
is like a year without summer.

-Swedish

Shared sorrow
is half sorrow.

-Danish

One enemy
is too many
and a hundred friends
are too few.

-Icelandic

You do not really know
your friends from your enemies
until the ice breaks.

-Icelandic (Eskimo)

Coming too close
can spoil a friendship.

-Swedish

After three days,
both fish and guests
begin to smell.

-Danish

A man's best friend
is his dog —
even better than his wife.

-Icelandic (Eskimo)

A man without a wife
is a man without thoughts.

-Finnish

He who beats his wife
beats his left hand
with his right.

-Danish

A woman's heart
sees more
than ten men's eyes.

-Swedish

He who takes the child
by the hand
takes the mother
by the heart.

-Danish

Midsummer night
is not long,
but it sets many cradles rocking.

-Swedish

One should choose
one's bedfellows
while it is daylight.

-Swedish

One cannot live on beauty,
but one can die for it.

-Swedish

Don't sail out
farther than you
can row back.

-Danish

He who lies on the floor
cannot fall down.

-Norwegian

Do not lift the club too high.
It may fall on your head.

-Finnish

When your neighbor's wall
breaks,
your own is in danger.

-Icelandic

Too little
or too much
spoils anything.

-Danish

Though your enemy
is the size of an ant,
regard him as an elephant.

-Danish

The wise man
is cheated only once.

-Finnish

What breaks in a moment
may take years to mend.

-Swedish

ONE CANNOT
SKI
SO SOFTLY
THAT
THE TRACES
CANNOT
BE SEEN.

-Finnish

The winter does not go
without looking backward.

-Finnish

Better a hawk in the hand
than two in flight.

-Icelandic

The echo knows all languages.

-Finnish

The steps
of the master
enrich
the field.

—Finnish

The twigs are rarely better
than the trunk.

—Icelandic

Hand washes hand
and
stone polishes stone.

—Icelandic

The water is the same
on both sides of the boat.

—Finnish

24

That which leaves no trace
has done no harm.

-Icelandic

Sweeter is the joy
that follows the
bitterness of fate.

-Danish

The light and the serious
go well together.

-Danish

God did not create hurry.

-Finnish

Everyone
finds his superior
once in a lifetime.

-Norwegian

You must be
in another man's power
to judge what he is worth.

-Danish

The nobler the blood,
the less the pride.

-Danish

Two
are an army
against one.

-Icelandic

*You cannot tell
a drunken man
from a madman
until both have slept.*

-Danish

*A bad haircut
is two people's shame.*

-Danish

LUCK is loaned, not owned.

-Norwegian

Bad
is called good
when worse happens.

-Norwegian

The afternoon knows
what the morning
never suspected.

-Swedish

If a man knew
where he would fall,
he would spread straw
there first.

-Finnish

Everyone
wants to live long,
but no one
wants to be called old.

-Icelandic

The thoughts of youth
are long, long thoughts.

-Finnish (Lapp)

The old man shows
what the young man was.

-Swedish

Being young
is a fault which diminishes daily.

-Swedish

He who lets the small things
                    bind him
leaves the great undone
                    behind him.

-Danish

This book may be brief,
but it's highly concentrated-
high-protein food for thought.
The last word is a proverb
from Iceland:

All old sayings
        have something in them.